T0170497

NORTHWEST
Readers

The Collected Poems of Ada Hastings Hedges

The
Collected Poems
of
Ada Hastings Hedges

EDITED BY

ALAN L. CONTRERAS

AND

ULRICH H. HARDT

WITH AN AFTERWORD BY

INGRID WENDT

Oregon State University Press   Corvallis

Library of Congress Cataloging-in-Publication Data

Names: Hedges, Ada Hastings, 1883–1980, author. | Contreras, Alan, 1956–
editor. | Hardt, Ulrich H., 1936– editor. | Wendt, Ingrid, 1944– writer
of afterword.
Title: The collected poems of Ada Hastings Hedges / edited by Alan L.
Contreras and Ulrich H. Hardt ; afterword by Ingrid Wendt.
Description: Corvallis : Oregon State University Press, 2020. | Series:
Northwest readers series | Includes bibliographical references and
index.
Identifiers: LCCN 2020005157 | ISBN 9780870719943 (trade paperback ; alk.
paper) | ISBN 9780870719950 (ebook)
Subjects: LCSH: Oregon–Poetry. | Sonnets, American.
Classification: LCC PS3515.E225 A6 2020 | DDC 811/.52—dc23
LC record available at https://lccn.loc.gov/2020005157

First published in 2020 by Oregon State University Press
Printed in the United States of America

Oregon State University Press
121 The Valley Library
Corvallis OR 97331
541-737-3166 • fax 541-737-3170
www.osupress.oregonstate.edu

The original source publication for each poem appears with the poem, when
known.

Title page photo of Ada Hastings Hedges courtesy Oregon State Library.

Series Preface

In 1990, the Oregon State University Press issued its first two books in the Northwest Reprint Series, *Oregon Detour* by Nard Jones, and *Nehalem Tillamook Tales*, edited by Melville Jacobs. Since then, the series has reissued a range of books by Northwest writers, both fiction and nonfiction, making available again works of well-known and lesser-known writers.

As the series developed, we realized that we did not always want to reissue a complete work; instead, we wanted to present selections from the works of a single author or selections from a number of writers organized around a unifying theme. Oregon State University Press, then, decided to start a new series, the Northwest Readers Series.

The reasons for the Northwest Readers Series are the same as for the Northwest Reprint Series: "In works by Northwest writers, we get to know about the place where we live, about each other, and about our history and culture."

Robert J. Frank, series editor

Dedicated to my friend Vjera, who appreciates the high desert as much as I do. —Alan

To Karen K. Johnson, this is affectionately dedicated. —Ulrich

Contents

DESERT POEMS (1930)

I. Alien

II. Wasteland

III. Sagebrush Village

IV. Silent Juniper

V. Desert Songs

VI. The Desert Wife

Poems 1933–1955

Acknowledgments

This publication grew out of several circumstances and conversations. We have enjoyed *Desert Poems* for many years. We were already familiar with C. E. S. Wood's *The Poet in the Desert* in its various iterations. Ada Hastings Hedges's approach to the same subject is both a significant free-standing addition to Oregon high-desert writing and, particularly in "The Desert Wife," a gentle reminder that although the high desert and its mountains can be a source of inspiration and mental challenge, the region is also an unforgiving partner.

Ingrid Wendt[1] provided early encouragement for this project and ideas about where to obtain Hedges's widely scattered output. Tim Lee and Noelle Moen helped track down copies of poems and related material from either obscure publications or archives not easily found through electronic searches. George Venn, one of Oregon's most knowledgeable literary historians, assisted with proofing and made useful suggestions regarding the biographical text.

Several other people helped with research into Hedges's life and the location of her work. We are grateful to Laura Golaszewski at the Normal (Illinois) Public Library; Holly Henning at Lake County Public Library in Leadville, Colorado; Kate Johnson in special collections archives at the University of Northern Colorado (formerly State Normal School), Greeley; and Matt Piersol at History Nebraska Archives in Lincoln,

Nebraska, for their invaluable assistance in helping us piece together information on the family and early years of Ada May Tyson Merrill Hastings Hedges.

We thank Bethany Barnes of the *Oregonian* for steering us to the paper's archives at the Multnomah County Library, where a number of poems were found, and to Josh Rodriguez, acquisitions program coordinator at the library, for making decades of bound hard copies available for our search. Likewise, thanks to Ryan Fernandez, Betsy Hammond, and Therese Bottomly from the *Oregonian* for assistance with permissions. Tamma Greenfield helped with the process of locating poems, as did her brother Sayre Greenfield. Nathan Williams, who has worked with Contreras on several other projects, retyped the entirety of *Desert Poems*.

We hope that modern readers will think our efforts worthwhile as they enjoy the work of this splendid poet.

Alan Contreras
Ulrich H. Hardt
September 2019

Introduction

Ada Hastings Hedges is an exquisite artist . . . one of the most finished poets in America. . . . —Borghild Lundberg Lee, poetry editor, the *Sunday Oregon Journal*, March 14, 1926[1]

She was born Ada May Tyson on December 18, 1883, on a small farm in the Glengary Precinct of Fillmore County, Nebraska. Her parents were Albert Mathias and Sarah Cora (Hastings) Tyson, who hailed from Illinois and Virginia respectively. They had an older daughter, Nellie Catherine, born in 1876, whose twin brother died in infancy. In June 1890, when Ada was six years old, Sarah divorced her husband, and on April 11, 1891, she married George W. Merrill, a mechanical engineer in Denver. Ada was adopted by her stepfather and used the name Ada May Merrill. The new family moved to Oro, a bustling gold mining town just outside of Leadville, Colorado, where George served as mining engineer, her mother kept house, and Ada thrived in school.

By 1900, her parents had moved to Portland, Oregon, and sixteen-year-old Ada was attending school and living with her older sister Nellie and her English-immigrant husband, Victor Chapman, a miner, in Lead, South Dakota. She graduated and applied for admission to Colorado State Normal School (now University of Northern Colorado) in Greeley in 1901, listing Leadville as her home. She earned a general education degree in 1904 and taught school in Fort Pierre, North Dakota, in 1905 and 1906.

We do not know how Ada Merrill met William Elias Hedges, a physician from Chicago eight years her senior, but they married on June 21, 1906. In 1910, Ada Hedges was living with Sarah and George Merrill in Portland and soon after, she and Dr. Hedges moved to the small community of Juntura, population 127, halfway between Burns and Vale on the Malheur River in southeastern Oregon's high desert, where he served as railroad doctor and she taught school for a time.

She published her first poems from Juntura in *Overland Monthly* in 1912 under the name Ada M. Hedges; in all work after that—published poems, newspaper columns, radio host, personal appearances—she used the name Ada Hastings Hedges, appropriating her mother's maiden name to honor her.

The 1920 census lists the Hedgeses living in Juntura. At the time of the 1930 census the couple lived in Los Angeles where he worked in the city's health department and she described herself as "author of short stories" and "wage worker." They settled back in Portland in 1932; she taught high school, and he practiced there until his death by heart attack in 1936. She was widowed at age fifty-two, and after his death became active in the veterans' rights movement—her husband was a World War I veteran. She served as supervising editor in the Works Progress Administration that produced *The WPA Guide to Oregon*, and she was assistant editor at Binfords & Mort Publishers.

The 1940 census shows Sarah C. Merrill (eighty-three) living with Ada in Portland. In 1951, Ada Hedges requested the University of Northern Colorado to send her 1904 transcripts to the Oregon superintendent of public instruction in Salem. Was she trying to renew her teaching license for public school teaching at age sixty-eight? We know that she last taught English literature and creative writing at Warner Pacific College, Portland, Oregon, in her early eighties from 1964 to1967.

Writing Career

The abiding interest in Hedges's life was writing: short fiction; a series of reviews of modern poetry, published in the *Albany Democrat*; and "Close-ups of Oregon Poets," which were presented on KOAC (Corvallis, Oregon) each Monday evening at 8:15 from 1932 to 1934. But most of all she wrote poetry. Oregon poet Ingrid Wendt has written that Hedges was one of the

Ada Hastings Hedges, from the 1941 *Spectator* (date of photo unknown).

first women's voices "to present alternative visions of human connection and continuity rooted in traditionally female values." Hedges had no children and passed her last three years in a Portland nursing home. She died July 8, 1980, and her remains are interred with her husband's at Portland Memorial.

This collection includes poems published from 1912 to 1955. Her first four poems appeared in four issues of *Overland Monthly* in 1912. When the *Sunday Oregon Journal* newspaper launched a new "Poets' Corner" in November 1924, four of Ada Hedges's poems were published during its first month, a sign of her prominence and popularity, as was her election as secretary of the Northwest Poetry Society the same year.

In her position as secretary, Hedges "expressed her vital interest in furthering the subject of poetry, the interests of the Northwest Poetry Society and individual

Ada Hastings Hedges in the Warner Pacific College 1965 yearbook (date of photo unknown).

poets."[2] In July 1932, she was elected treasurer of the Oregon branch of the American Fiction Guild, a professional writers' association organized by president Albert Richard Wetjen, editor of the *Oregon Magazine* and prominent Oregon writer of sea stories and novels. Alfred Powers in his 1935 *History of Oregon Literature* hailed her as a worthy representative of Northwest poets.[3] That she was still promoting poetry more than a dozen years later is echoed in the November 20, 1938, announcement that Hedges, newly appointed editor at Binfords & Mort Publishers, represented "a break for Northwest writers!"[4] Among her first assignments there was editing Richard I. Helm's 1938 novel, *Blue Waters.*

However, Hedges was not a prolific poet. Poems, she felt, must be carefully presented and with emotional justification to qualify as poetry. Far too many "poems" in her day did not qualify. They may have had authentic beginnings but "wrecked themselves on the rocks of craftsmanship." Accomplished poets keep their ideas in their minds for a long time, examine them at intervals, wait for them to gather power before they even attempt to put them down. Finding words for their meaning, that is what should occupy poets—altering words to suit meaning and modifying meaning to satisfy the requirements of their words. She was fond of quoting Edna St. Vincent Millay, who admonished young poets to write and rewrite poems and never to be satisfied with what they had written first.

Hedges did not hesitate to criticize so prominent a fellow Portland poet and critic as Eleanor MacMillan: "So lovely an idea should have been given a beautiful body, by which is meant, of course, a more enduring form," she said of MacMillan's poem "Reflections." "If a rhyme is forced, ever so slightly, it is not artistic nor finished work and does not deserve the name of poetry. All words must fall naturally as they would in the most artistic prose, and the rhyme must seem inevitable."[5]

Poetry remained undefinable for her. She liked Robert Frost's notion that "a poem begins with a lump in the throat," and Sara Teasdale's idea that "poems are written because of an emotional irritation," something felt—and thought out afterwards. In other words, a poem finds its way from the feeling into thought, and from thought into the words.

In her poems we also see modifications in style. Content, she thought, must always remain the most important consideration, but style has its own significance, and the most striking transformation in her style was in diction. Her poems are distinctive in the way she used language, with sincerity and directness, and without sentimentality. Gone is the concern with creed, replaced by the concern with truth. Hedges was not so much concerned with her relation to the infinite as with that between individuals and their material surroundings.

As a result, her poetry is not lofty or top-heavy as is much of the work of her contemporaries. She did not rhapsodize but used ordinary words in daily use for their beauty and strength. In giving up inflated rhetorical diction for speech that is commonly heard, Hedges gained a new distinction and sincerity. Though displaying a complexity of vision, her poems are readable and understood by average people, because they can feel the words. Turn, at random, to any of her poems for examples of this. Poetry loses its vitality if words are used according to a set formula.

Desert Poems
One of the few authors associated with the wide expanse of the southeastern high desert of Oregon, Hedges published her only collection, *Desert Poems*, in 1930. She told Alfred Powers that the desert region had always fascinated her; she had "found it full of mystery and beauty in its own bleak fashion . . . strangely haunting and baffling, as a forest surely has a consciousness different from that of a mountain or the sea." The hills impacted her with "their austerity and their strength." When a critic accused her of including too little color in her desert, she shot back, "I could give it only as I saw it."[6] These desert poems were written in traditional sonnet form, but from a feminist point of view,

"informed by the acridness of the rough-edged railroad and cattle town Juntura and the surrounding sagebrushed lava-miles . . . indifferent and timeless as the stars."

"The Desert Wife"

With her most famous sequence of poems, thirteen sonnets entitled "The Desert Wife," which are included in *Desert Poems*, Hedges can be described as the 'other' poet in the Oregon desert, because in these poems she in effect responds to C. E. S. Wood's *The Poet in the Desert* (1915, rev. 1918 and 1929). Wood saw the desert as something to be subdued or seduced, or perhaps as a place to escape to from urban life. Hedges knew it as a symbol of an awesome, terrifying, and indifferent cosmos, and she is powerless to change her fate within it. She speaks for those Oregon pioneers who made their home in the "promised land" of the high desert, describing the toll this took on their lives:

> They grew more passive with the meagre years,
> Upon their lips and hearts the desert lay
> The silence that had throbbed upon their ears—
> And after all there was not much to say.
> (Sonnet XII)

In Hedges's most admired poems, she follows the Shakespearean sonnet metric and rhyme, but because the poems are narratives, they lack the internal logic of Shakespeare's. However, Hedges retains the Elizabethan model by embedding in the concluding couplet the narrative core and the tone of the preceding twelve lines. Sometimes this happens with ironic intensification. In sonnet VIII, after the wife responded to the terrors lurking in the landscape—the "mystery at its cinder core . . . an ultimate power . . . crouched like a tawny beast"—she sought her husband's comfort, not out of love, but from fear: "the weird coyote's midnight bark sent her to his pillow in the dark."

Ada Hedges's care with composition explains the gap in her publication record between 1913 and 1923, which overlaps with the period 1910 to 1920 during which she lived in Juntura in Malheur County. She was not ready to publish her remarkable *Desert Poems* until a decade later.

It was not until after the publication of *Desert Poems* that Ethel Romig Fuller, longtime poetry editor of the *Oregonian,* could answer the question, "Who and how good are Oregon poets?" In a major *Sunday Oregonian* article on November 19, 1933, she explains: "Not too difficult a task, since we do have today in the Northwest a genuine and distinctive regional poetry . . . with Portland as a pivot in becoming the ultimate literary center of the country."

Fuller then quotes Pulitzer Prize–winning poet John Gould Fletcher, who agrees:

> Culture does not exist in New York . . . but in the void, out of relation to what the rest of the world may say or do or think. In the fine, vigorous verse of our present-day Oregon poets we have authentic voices, poets who have made Oregon's tradition theirs in the highest sense, in such lines as Ada Hastings Hedges writes:
>
>> "The desert has its sorrows: dust for dreams
>> Of mist and trees to soften each contour
>> Too sharply drawn—of showers and of streams
>> Implacably withheld by some old foe;
>> And somewhere in these hills must still endure
>> A hunger such as only deserts know."[7]

Hedges was considered a leading poet in her time. In November 1925, Gwladys Bowen, book editor of the *Oregon Journal,* announced that Hedges—along with Ellinor Norcross, Ethel Romig Fuller, and Howard McKinley Corning—had "been given the signal and national honor of being included in William Stanley Braithwaite's *Anthology of Magazine Verse for 1925*, an attainment which all poets strive for and few attain." Her poem, "Autumn Evening," "an exquisite lyric, . . . stands out in beauty and individuality."[8]

Fellow poet Howard McKinley Corning, an early admirer of Hedges's work, wrote in the *Sunday Oregon Journal* that

> In the midst of our disparagement of the poetic voice comes this poem in *Contemporary Verse*: "Autumn in the Desert" ["The Desert III," p. 59] by Ada Hastings Hedges. Here is a cross section of the desert, that is feeling as well as seeing, a poem that has grown out of its source into voice. It is indigenous, and not a laying on of mental coloring and dexterous word usage. It is really a most creditable poem, though too solid with substance for the mass mind to enjoy. The pity of good poetry, the better it gets the slimmer its appreciating audience. The light, homely lyric is the popular poetry. Let us have more of such authentic singing as this quoted sonnet.[9]

Ada Hedges was in the public eye through her engagement in literary societies, her editorial work, and her circle of friends. Her astute and frank columns in the *Albany Democrat* newspaper reached a wide audience, and she was invited to give talks and readings. She did not play the role so often associated with women poets, writing sentimental verse on domestic subjects. Oh, she could and did write a number of love poems in which she raptures: "Seen through the prism of your love my days / Are rainbow-hued . . . / . . . Bathed in this translucent flame / My life's poor sequence, pale as desert sands / Has broken into iridescent bands." ("Spectrum," p. 45) But always, as in "Summer's End" (p. 115), the reader is brought back to stark reality:

Love, too, has both its green and barren bough—
And when these leaves are blown across the hill
And scattered by the winds that stir them now,
In greater girth, more deeply rooted still,
This tree will lift its naked branches high—
So, stripped of love, I face the winter sky.

A year after her husband's death, in "Then April" (p. 124), Hedges struggles to deal with acceptance of reality:

I saw the silent golden leaves
Fall from the autumn pear,
With sorrow for a summer's end,
A bough of love left bare.

And ultimately, in the closing line of "Finale" (p. 125), she shows us how to move to final resignation: "For all is mutable, and all must pass."

Oregon Poets in the Spotlight

In a much-anticipated visit, Harriet Monroe, influential editor of *Poetry*, came to Portland on March 27, 1926. The members of the Northwest Poetry Society were abuzz with excitement to hear the "spinsterish little lady, standing on the bare platform, intoning her correctly-worded and carefully-modulated lines, little affected by her precise lyricism or her studied intellectuality. But she was 'there,' while we were only beginners with a consuming urge for self-expression," recalled society president Corning.[10]

That evening, in a home of one of the group on Council Crest, Monroe graciously listened to a reading of poetry by what she had by now christened "The Portland Group," and urged them on with the comment: "You'll make *Poetry* someday." And so they did. Corning in 1926 and Hedges in 1927 were the first. The

November 1927 issue of *Poetry* published Hedges's "Now" (p. 48) and "Release" (p. 85) (*Poetry* 31, no. 2, 79). Others of the group followed—Ethel Romig Fuller, Borghild Lundberg Lee, Verne Bright, Queene Lister, and Charles Oluf Olsen.

The *Portland Telegram* called them an "insurgent group" because of their success in shifting control of the well-known New Verse scene of back East to the more relevant Northwest Poetry Society, which was leading the renaissance. Even Harriet Monroe had to admit that during her visit, and Hedges with her influential column in the Albany newspaper played no small role in this development. She also published poems in the *Commonweal* and the *Nation* soon after *Poetry*.

"Portland claims—we hope with becoming modesty—to be the third city in the United States in actual (not per capita) numbers of nationally known writers, with New York, first, and Hollywood, second," wrote Ethel Romig Fuller in the Preface of Henry Harrison's *Oregon Poets: An Anthology of 50 Contemporaries* (1935). "If 'Portland, Oregon' were to be printed after the name of each Oregon author, as his, or her [work] appeared in current magazines . . . the roster would be an imposing one."[11] Hedges had five poems in this anthology, notably only one from *Desert Poems* ("Silent Juniper," p. 87), the others selected from magazines and newspapers.

Commentators in *Northwest Books* (1942) noted that Hedges wrote "lyrics of distinguished literary quality and appeal," and they praised the desert poems in particular for their "diction, beauty, and depth of understanding."[12] As noted above, Alfred Powers singled out her work for mention among contemporary Oregon poets in his *History of Oregon Literature* in 1935. Frederick Woodward Skiff called her a "keen student of human nature."[13]

The *Oregon Journal*'s poetry editor, Borghild Lee, wrote that Hedges "is an exquisite artist . . . one of the most finished poets in America."[14] Lee also wrote in her review of *Desert Poems* in the *Spectator* that

Oregon writers, 1928. Back (l to r): Ada Hastings Hedges, Charles Alexander, Elizabeth Olsen, Ethel Romig Fuller, Borghild (Peggy) Lee, Floyd Dell, Mrs. Charles Alexander, Verne Bright, Queene Lister; front: Charles Olsen, Howard McKinley Corning, and Alexander's daughter, Cloris. Photo originally published in *Oregon Historical Quarterly* 73, no. 4 (December 1972).

here is no ordinary verse, but poetry in the truest sense of the word. For the sheer esthetic pleasure of reading flowing musical lines, these poems cannot be surpassed. The technique is flawless, but one is never aware of the fine workmanship.... The emotion, the idea and the form are blended to a perfect whole, and one is only aware of music of mellow beauty.[15]

Corning, president of the Oregon State Poetry Association and poetry editor of the *Oregonian* from 1965 to 1976, gave this detailed and insightful description of his contemporary in 1973:

Ada Hastings Hedges was quiet of manner and soft of voice. Always she spoke with a studied choice of words, seldom with assertive statements, and when speaking surveyed you with frank, steady expression, as if watching to see if you would accept her words with the same honesty with which they were being uttered. Her eyes were gray. Her hair, with some curl, was, in those early years, lighter than chestnut. As a person, she seemed to me wholly self-contained, and with a depth of spirit not discernible among others of my acquaintance. This spiritual quality identified all that she wrote, particularly her poems which were drawn from the moody Eastern Oregon desert landscape and life. She wrote lyrics, many in the sonnet form, some of them character studies. She too made *Poetry* and the *Nation,* the *London Mercury,* the *Commonweal,* and others.[16]

Hedges's poems were sufficiently well known to be borrowed for use in other publications, for example in a 1977 history of the Oregon hamlet of Millican. Stewart H. Holbrook in his 1945 *Promised Land: A Collection of Northwest Writing* includes Hedges's "Desert Road" (p. 70) as "a typical sample of what Northwest writers have been doing in the past twenty years. . . . Mrs. Hedges's verse, often inspired by her eight [*sic*] years of residence in the desert country of eastern Oregon, has appeared in leading American and English magazines."[17]

Ada Hedges was measured in what she published. To Borghild Lundberg Lee she confided that "of modern poetry—there is plenty of it. But much of it seems without justification. So little of it worthwhile. One feels a sense of futility, if not guilt, in attempting to produce more verse."[18]

Modern Views
Today, Hedges is remembered mainly for "The Desert Wife" and the desert poems in general. Among those who have a broad knowledge of Oregon poetry, her work continues to stand out for its richness of diction, connection to the land, and technical competence. Modern anthologies have selected work by Hedges

as representative of American poetry. A selection from "Desert Road" (p. 70) was used as recently as 2017 in *The United States in Literature*.[19] George Venn, in recent correspondence with the editors, notes that

> On that arid, Paiute, agrarian frontier, she sojourned for more than ten years, internalizing a lifetime of conflicting images, refining her poetic craft, and developing a formal dualistic aesthetic.
>
> By the time she returned to Portland after 1920, the sonnet had become her most trusted, complex, and acute lens for exploring and expressing difference, otherness, and opposites. Unlike the expansive Whitmanesque lines of C. E. S. Wood's *Poet in the Desert* (1915), Hedges rendered the dreams, agonies, endurance, triumphs, losses, and defeats of men and women in classic meters and rhythms.

The poems in this collection continue to inspire, as demonstrated in the rare hand-colored selection from *Desert Poems* issued by Philoxenia Press in Berkeley, California, in 2014. Norman McKnight is the gifted artist who produced this volume. McKnight grew up partly in eastern Oregon in the 1950s, attended the University of Oregon for a time and is, today, a highly respected letterpress printer and artist in Berkeley, California. Fourteen copies on lush paper were hand-colored and bound for sale. The work was, alas, sold out by 2019.

The Poems

When a book of poems from a long-gone poet is called "collected," the question of completeness arises—the nature of poetry publication leaves the possibility of stray sheep. This was especially true during the heyday of small magazines in the early twentieth century when Hedges wrote. Some of the journals where she is known to have published still exist, but others do not. Many more have probably disappeared and have taken her work with them, awaiting a scholarly dredging beyond the scope of this book. It is difficult to find older material in newspapers and journals that have no indexes, even on paper, and, in some cases, are not even in the United States. Therefore, this is a volume of *collected* poems, not the *complete* poems. We trust that readers will be glad for the eighty-nine poems we have found and printed here, including forty-six poems not in *Desert Poems*.

In addition to *Desert Poems*, the only collection published during her lifetime, Hedges's poems appeared in the *Oregonian*, *Oregon Journal*, and major periodicals, such as the *Nation*, *Commonweal*, *Poetry*, the *New York Times*, *London Mercury*, and *Contemporary Verse*. Her work also appeared in a host of popular magazines and local newspapers, such as *Sunset* and the *Albany Democrat*. As far as we have been able to determine, she published her first poem in *Overland Monthly* in 1912 at age twenty-eight and her last in 1955 in the *Oregonian*, at age seventy-one. However, we know that she continued writing, if not publishing, into her nineties. At age ninety-six, shortly before her death, she received an honorable mention for a poem she entered in the annual Ben Hur Lampman poetry contest. We have not been able to locate that poem.

Technical Issues

The poems are presented here in chronological order, with one grouped exception. All of the poems in *Desert Poems* are reprinted together as they appeared in the original, published in the year 1930. In some cases, poems included in *Desert Poems* had appeared earlier under another title. If this information is known, it is included in a note.

Poems that have been revised but are clearly based in the same work, e.g., "Bequest," are provided in both versions. In a couple of cases, "Mist" and "Desert Spring"/"The Desert," a slightly revised version appeared in another venue.

Poems printed in newspapers were often restricted to very narrow columns that generated forced enjambments without a syntactical purpose or effect, sometimes a long string of lines in which the last word was artificially pushed to the next line for no apparent reason. These have been corrected in this collection when they are reasonably obvious. Hedges did not generally scatter her words about—indeed, 56 percent of the poems in this collection are written in sonnet form—so it is unlikely that problems have been created here.

If it is clear in the original that line breaks are intended (e.g., as in "Sleep, Stay Your Step," p. 46), then those breaks are retained. Hedges generally used some kind of formal structure, so the poem "Nocturne" (p. 122) stands out for its unique streaming flow. Endnotes are provided when a reader may be confused by a particular line layout. We hope that readers will forgive the occasional visual infelicities that these various adjustments created.

The editors have made every reasonable effort to trace the ownership of copyrighted material and to make full acknowledgment of its use. If errors or omissions have occurred, they will be corrected in subsequent editions, provided that notification is submitted in writing to the publisher.

The editors consider Ada Hastings Hedges to be one of Oregon's best poets and an underappreciated part of our poetic history. We are happy to bring her work before new audiences.

Alan L. Contreras, Eugene, Oregon
Ulrich H. Hardt, Portland, Oregon

Reprinted by permission of the *Oregonian*. Courtesy OHS Research Library, CN011423

Hedges on the Nature of the Poetic Arts

In January 1925, Portland poet and critic Howard McKinley Corning (later the poetry editor for the *Oregonian*—1965–1976) opened a discussion in the *Oregon Journal* on the question, "Are poets born or made?" His strong contention was, "Poetry cannot be taught." His essay unleashed weeks of vigorous argument in the newspaper, and on February 25, 1925, Ada Hastings Hedges weighed in with her opinion.

Her well-argued, nine-hundred-word essay sheds light on how she approached poetry, informed, no doubt, by her training and her practice as a teacher. Her study of older and contemporary poets led her to conclude that there are few born poets, that "the miracle almost never happens." In her essay, she eventually comes "to the middle ground." Born with the necessary gifts, the master poets have learned to make the most of their endowments and to "hear" their inspirations. "Poets must be born—and made."

Corning, in his rebuttal at the end of the wide-ranging, weeks-long public symposium on March 22, 1925, is obliged to admit that readers "can do nothing better than to re-read Ada Hastings Hedges's contribution," because she is a poet and has "brooked the fine edge that is poetry's province" on the question.

We are pleased to reprint Hedges's essay here, by way of introducing her own work.

Can Poetry Be Taught?

Once upon a time I supposed that poets were all born. They sang spontaneously and perfectly and gloriously from the very beginning. In the light of what has been gathered, both from the poets, who have been able to tell how they have done it, and from their work itself, this belief has been modified. A comparison of the earlier and the later works of poets, especially of the contemporary poets, is a fascinating and a revealing study. It leads me to the middle ground of this discussion, that poets must be born—and made. They must be born and they must be made. The two theories are not irreconcilable. The art of poetry not only can be taught, but it is invariably taught, though its divine essence is a gift of the gods.

Poets come into the world trailing their clouds of natural endowment. They come with the emotional temperament, the creative fervor, the musical perception, the native rhythm, the sense of proportion, the winged imagination, the sensitiveness of beauty, the passion for truth and the spiritual insight to perceive it, and above all, the impelling necessity for utterance. That they are in possession of these poetic gifts, and many more, is presupposed. This equipment cannot be taught, but it can be unfolded, and cultivated, and trained to function. When nicely balanced with an instrument capable of perfect utterance, we have the poet born. The two rarely coincide. The miracle almost never happens.

But we do have something else that is often overlooked. It is the tendency of genius to remain latent. It does not manifest as fluently as most of us suppose. Educational systems do not recognize this fact. Too often they are concerned with the veneer, the attempt to add something from the outside instead of dealing with fundamental constructive processes. The argument against the teaching of poetry has not gone back far enough. It must take into consideration something more than the superficial aspects of the question. The teaching of poetry, as I see it, is not merely the presentation of the rules of versification. It is also making available to the potential poet all of his latent powers. Let us suppose, for instance, that we do not begin with maturity in our methods, but with the children of the fifth or sixth grades, or earlier, and that we attempt to teach them to express themselves rhythmically instead of following the course of study which requires them to memorize certain classics of poetry. I believe that we might uncover many geniuses that are otherwise lost to the world through the inhibition of our present mode of training. I do not mean that the memory work is not important. It develops literary appreciation and cultivates taste, and drill work also has its place.

Genius is often dammed behind barriers that can be broken down by training. Many individuals have the poetic endowment without being wholly conscious of it. They can be taught to explore themselves for gifts that have not come to the surface. Genius may be more of a habit than we suspect.

This is what the master poets have done, often by accident. All the great poets, in one way or another, have been taught poetry. While all great poetry must, in a sense, make itself, it is not a matter of chance. "Poems that just come," as Edwin Markham has it, "should usually be returned whence they came." Poets do not toss off their songs after the manner of a meadow lark from the fence post. Engaging as this superstition is, I have been forced to lay it aside—not without a pang of disillusionment.

A few may learn to produce rapidly, but only after they have done a vast amount of practice work. Poetry is a slow growth. It is learned only after years of laborious discipline, years of writing, and re-writing and discarding. Prosaic as it may seem, they have learned their craft much as a tailor has learned to fashion garments. Consciously or otherwise, every poet must live through some such educational process, evolving his craftsmanship from within. In no other way can they make their moods communicable.

The years when Edgar Lee Masters was groping about were a vocational education. But no one would have suspected him of being a poet in the days of his "Hail to thee" verse. It did not make him any the less a genius, however, because he had not yet come into the kingdom of his endowment.

The educational process will reveal its failures, too. In Amy Lowell, we have a fairly good example of the attempt to make a poet. She has taught herself to function in meter and rhythm—sometimes, but that which is produced as a matter of craftsmanship, cannot be called poetry.

But thousands of potential poets will remain mute and inglorious to the end of the chapter, not through any lack of endowment, but because it was not accessible, or they were hampered by the limitations of instruction. Their inspirations may be as fine as any that are voiced, if we could but hear them. No one has a monopoly on inspiration, but the master poet will be able to give expression to his. Because when the emotion comes—the reaction to the pleasure or pain, he will be ready. Born with the necessary gifts, he has learned to make the most of them.

Ada Hastings Hedges, 1925

POEMS
1912–1929

SANCTUARY

A place of pillared silence, dim
　　And cool—of holy solitude—
Far off it is, and deep within
　　The tranquil wood.

Worn, dust-choked in the blinding noon,
　　I flee from noisy care a space,
And find here in the firs' grey gloom
　　A resting place.

Secure at last from clamoring strife,
　　Amid the wind-chant's soothing roll,
The columned firs breathe fragrant life
　　To prostrate soul.

At length serene and trustingly
　　I go, from fear all disenthralled—
Content to meet my destiny
　　And unappalled.[1]

Overland Monthly, March 1912

Daybreak in June

Rose petals lightly strewn
  All over the dewy lawn:
Across the sky in soft festoon
  Rose petal clouds of dawn!

Overland Monthly, May 1912

To Mount St. Helens

Elusive as the ling'ring morning mist,
　　With outlines dimly traced against the sky,
Thy summit stands serene, unchangingly,
　　Cloud-white with everlasting snows that lie
Upon thy far, faint crest.

To us who dwell below and heedless plod
　　The days, and half-achieving, hurry on,
Impart the secret of thy timeless calm—
　　Tell us, does that undying quiet come
From close proximity to God?

Overland Monthly, June 1912

AMONG THE FIRS

When I am far away from this,
And weary of the din,
That throbs and beats and whirls all day
Out in the world of men;

When I look out upon the throng
With undiscerning eye—
Come back to me when hope is dead,
A healing memory.

Blow, then, this pungent breath to me!
And weariness shall cease;
Once more the benediction fall
Of this hour's perfect peace.

Overland Monthly, August 1912

Homeland

So many days my seeking heart
    Went roving alien skies,
When all the while the thing it sought
    Lay hidden in your eyes.

The empty days, the lonely nights
    That I have journeyed through
And always—always you were here
    And yet I never knew!

I did not know—I did not dream—
    But oh, the weary quest
Has only made more dear to me
    The haven of your breast.

Out West and *Overland Monthly*, May 1924

If You Had Died

If there had been a sudden silence blown
    Upon that hour—I say, if you had died
When Love was at its glorious flowing tide,
Thrilling and terrible—I should have known
The wistful savor of a gentle grief
Haunting my moods—a fragile, silver blight
To stain my landscape like the muted light
Upon a cloud-dimmed day; and yet belief
That you would wait beyond the barrier
Warm at my heart. I could have gone each day
Beneath my standard gallantly the way
Of secret peace, immune from this wide blur
Of sand left on an empty, listless shore
Whose tides have strangely ebbed to come no more.[2]

Lyric West, November, 1924.
Reprinted in *Sunday Albany Democrat*, January 11, 1925

Captivity

Birds in the stormy dusk
    Circle the sky;
Lonely as wind and lost
    Bewildered they fly.

On their swift, fearless wings
    I should be gone,
Far from November skies
    To some spring dawn.[3]

Sunday Oregon Journal, November 16, 1924

November

One day, their wistful branches bare and dumb,
The poplars stood against the grey March skies—
The next, they swarmed with buds, like little cries
Of joy, crowding the boughs—and spring had come;
Had come, as always childish with delight
At our surprise to find the poplar lane
Dimmed by a floating mist of green again.
And then came summer, rising to its height
Of loveliness—and autumn, as the flow
And ebb of tides. And through the moving year,
It seemed that any hour might bring you here
To share it all; but now I know—I know!
Three seasons passed in song above my head,
Before I could believe that you are dead.

Sunday Oregon Journal, November 16, 1924

On the Hill

A little from the city's restless sea
We found a wooded slope, where through the shade
Of singing firs, its distant murmur strayed,
A deep-toned voice, hushed to their pensive key.
October-tinted leaves dropped silently:
Like these, our bright-winged moments, too, were made
To pass, and yet for us they may not fade—
These flaming fragments of eternity.

When twilight fell, the lights came out below,
As stars through mist in some inverted sky,
And lost among them in that web of blue,
Were two small waiting lights. And in the slow,
Chill dusk, we saw the sunset splendor die—
Two separate stars were calling—me from you!

Sunday Oregon Journal, November 16, 1924

Reading from Chesterton

Your eyes grew deep and dreaming as you listened
To cadences that crashed like thunder out of space;
I lost the thrilling splendor of the story—
Forgotten was the very time and place—
I lost myself among the brooding shadows
That crossed like clouds the quiet of your face.

Sunday Oregon Journal, December 14, 1924

FAREWELL [in memory of Hazel Hall]

Though it is spring, you do not wait to see,
Like mist from earth, spring rise immaculate
To drift from hill to hill, from tree to tree—
For earth's supreme white mood, you do not wait.
They do not keep you—not the swaying bough
That bears its beauty tentative as snow,
Not wild syringa—not the dogwood now—
This is the sorrow that the heart must know.

Spring is not lost, for this intense white hour
Is yours forever—past our dark distrust;
The cool white texture that you loved, the flower,
The stainless bough will never turn to dust;
Graven it is in memory so deep—
Forever yours beyond this marble sleep.[4]

A Tribute to Hazel Hall, Caxton (1939)

Sleep, Stay Your Feet

Sleep, stay your sandaled feet
    That darkness brings,
Soft as the measured beat
    Of twilight wings.

Others will seek till dawn
    Forgetfulness—
Grant them oblivion
    By your caress.

In this your tender guise
    Find grief laid bare,
With your cool touch close eyes
    Upon despair.

Down your dim aisles of rest
    Let others stray
If at this day's curved crest
    I still may stay.[5]

Sunday Oregon Journal, February 15, 1925

Resurgence

I hear them pass my window in the night,
The little ghosts of Aprils that we knew—
Over the hills they trail their robes of white,
And through the dark my hands reach out to you.
Men call it Spring; to me it is a name
To mark a season with—a cycle done;
For since the wind that blew away Life's flame.
The almond trees may blossom in the sun
And hawthornes gladden every lane, for me
Spring does not come. These silver days wind by
Tarnished and dim, like waters to the sea
Across the furrowed, empty sands while I
Fance dawns where eagerly beyond the gates
Of some clear, unborn day it waits . . . it waits![6]

Muse & Mirror, 1924

Then April!

I came through long grey days of peace
    Unwinding like a thread,
With ghostly steps that should have paused
    Among the dreamless dead.

But these things brought life throbbing back
    With one swift stab of pain—
Wet fragrance from a lilac tree,
    A bird song through the rain![7]

Sunday Oregon Journal, April 4, 1925

A Woman

I did not know how fragile they could be,
These quickly squandered, scattered hours of bliss—
Too brief and fugitive a dream was this
To leave immutable its legacy
Of sorrow throbbing as the rhythms run
Through song, the flame of hunger that must go
Unfed to embers, and the tread of slow
Dark days across the brightness of the sun.

After the shipwreck I at length may rest,
Cast here upon my empty, desert isle,
And know that this wide loneliness is best—
Glad of the sullen breakers, mile on mile,
Glad of the refuge from the sea and gale—
Scanning the gray horizon for a sail.

Sunday Oregon Journal, June 7, 1925

Not for This

You are an alien wanderer, a dream
Woven of tapestries of tender Junes
In stately gardens, with the sapphire gleam
Of fountains playing under silver moons.
You lost your way from an old-gold romance,
Framed in the splendor of a castle hall—
Betrayed by some indifferent circumstance
Upon a dusty path where shadows fall.

Sometimes I read deep in your grave sweet eyes,
Where half-remembered things are slumbering yet,
The troubled stirring of a hurt surprise;
Sometimes I think that you do not forget,
But meant to come beneath a kindlier star—
Child of a fairy tale—how lost you are!

Sunday Oregon Journal, June 21, 1925

ENLIGHTENMENT

Some other day when autumn winds are swaying
These boughs uplifted to the somber skies.
Immune to drifting leaves I shall be straying
Down lanes of peace, grown strangely sure and wise.
I'll stand within the castle of your dreaming,
Whose walls rise now to stay my eager feet;
With this dark exile I shall be redeeming
The sunlight when the cycle is complete.
I'll find the words that never have been spoken,
That circled softly near us for a while.
I'll know when these brave barriers are broken
The hidden things that lie beneath your smile;
If this is you or some disguise you wear—
I'll know, my dear, when I no longer care.

Sunday Oregon Journal, October 25, 1925

Autumn Evening

Now that the early rains have brought once more
    The firelight and the intimate, sheltered gloom
Of curtains drawn, a charm not known before
    Dwells in the shadows of my quiet room.
Moving against the murmur of the rain,
    The velvet rustle of the wood-flame weaves
A subtle harmony, while down the pane
    There comes the vagrant splash of dripping leaves.

In this immediate peace there is no word
    That for some deep and strangely scented night
In June, old loneliness shall be deferred;
    Even the certainty has taken flight
That there is yet a tryst I shall fulfill
    With heartbreak waiting on an April hill.

Sunday Oregon Journal, November 1, 1925

Finale

Now that I have come to empty days
Whose quiet is unstirred and strangely new,
Too quiet and too strange is this grey peace
Where swirls no gusty memory of you.

Remembering so the tumult of the wind
That has swept by, a lonely, old tree grieves
Through long December silences and chill,
For the lost rapture of its shaken leaves.[8]

Sunday Oregon Journal, November 8, 1925

INTERVAL

And now for one love more or less
I do not care at all—
There is a path at the water's edge
Where red leaves fall.

From restless days a pause has come,
From dreams, a cool release,
While I rest my eyes with a hill's curve,
And my heart with peace.

Sunday Oregon Journal, December 6, 1925

Alien

Whenever April walks upon the hill
    Among her own white secrets in the dew,
Where slender shadows sway and then grow still,
    Beneath the boughs that dream against the blue—
I know that in another land of dim
    Horizons reaching lonely as the sea,
Where a sagebrush flattens over sand, a grim
    Peace dwells neutral to river, bird or tree.

And if no singing seasons ever come
    Down some long hill they love to loiter on;
If these grey slopes of sorrow must be dumb
    Of dreams forever, if from dawn to dawn,
A wind shall murmur through the desert grass—
One need not see another April pass.[9]

Sunday Oregon Journal, March 28, 1926

ALIEN

This reach of sagebrush with its windy hill
Framed by my doorway, is a troubled place
Known only to my dreams, remembered still
In daylight hours to haunt them for a space.
In some azalea-scented dark once more,
Where swans are drifting down a quiet lake,
Curving their silver arc along the shore.

And faintly now I almost thought I heard—
As one would hear across the verge of sleep—
Out of the grey wind's sudden lull, in bars
Of gold, the slender rapture of a bird—
A rift of joy that no wild throat could keep,
Taking its flight among the listening stars.[10]

Commonweal, June 9, 1926

Spectrum

Seen through the prism of your love my days
Are rainbow-hued. The lovely coloring
Tinges with radiance the humblest thing
I do; and all small joys beneath its rays
Kindle to rapture. With still stranger powers
It filters bitterness from tears and stains
Old griefs to gentle sadness, as the panes
Of rich-toned glass transmute the light to showers
Of beauty. Bathed in this translucent flame
My life's poor sequence, pale as desert sands,
Has broken into iridescent bands
Of splendor, gold and purple hours reclaim
Its shady solitudes and lure my feet
Toward dawns that grow more luminous and sweet.

Sunset, October 1926

SLEEP, STAY YOUR STEP

Sleep, stay your sandaled feet;
    With your soft tread
Come silences to meet
    Above my head.

Let not your shadow fall
    Upon me, Sleep,
Obliterating all
    That I would keep.

Many will seek till dawn
    Forgetfulness;
Grant them oblivion
    With your caress.

And in your tender guise
    Find grief laid bare.
With your cool touch close eyes
    Upon despair. . . .

Down your dim aisles of rest
    Let others stray.
If at this day's curved crest
    I still may stay. [11]

New York Times, July 21, 1927

BEQUEST

This was your dream, to give the desert song—
    A lilac tree for April when it came;
An almond mist to shimmer through the long
    Spring twilights, and for Autumn days the flame
Of maples flung to the wind in gay
    Surrender; and as if to fortify
Your heart, a poplar lane to veil the gray
    And lonely reaches of the land and sky.
The sterile earth lay silent and inert,
    Until beneath your wistful touch it grew
Articulate with things kept from the hurt
    Of frost and sun by tender ways you knew.
And now Spring tarries longer, year by year,
Because an exile with a dream was here.[12]

New York Times, August 22, 1927

Now

Not for my spirit's sake, I said;
My spirit's hunger may be fed—
My spirit that shall find no bars
On other quests to other stars;
And like a gull from some dark stream,
Its flight shall widen dream by dream:

But for this flesh whose pulses beat
Their wistful rhythm of defeat—
This gallant flesh that shall lie still
In long surrender on a hill,
Learning utterly, as it must,
The lonely destiny of dust—
I take this hour, this hour, I said;
My body's hunger must be fed.[13]

Poetry, November 1927

MIST

The hills are dimmed to memories, in tiers
The town, a blue dream, turns to aging stone;
And all is blurred, as something seen through years,
That once was definite and near and known.
Like rapture time has reaped, the soft mist holds
The gold and rapture time scarlet of each separate tree—
A frozen mountain lost among its folds,
A river widening slowly to the sea.
The mist is passionless—it cools and stills
The fevers that are borne for beauty's sake;
With autumn flaming on a hundred hills,
It stills the heart that otherwise must break. . . .
I love the mist that keeps the soul secure
From more of earth than it could well endure.[14]

Commonweal, October 1928

Summer

If there should come a wet wind from the sea
To freshen at the heart these hills that parch
Beneath the sun, and if more tenderly
The light should fall from the relenting arch
Of sky, or shadow cooled by rain should fold
In silver mist these broken slopes, subdue
And comfort them, their naked breasts might hold
The peace of forests, dim and veiled and blue.

The desert has its sorrows; dust for dreams
Of mist and trees to soften each contour
Too sharply drawn—of showers and of streams
Implacably withheld by some old foe;
And somewhere in these hills must still endure
A hunger such as only deserts know.

Nation, September 18, 1929

DESERT POEMS
1930

≈ ≈ ≈

"The tragedy, the futility, the eternal struggle against the desert is told with utter sincerity and compelling power. . . ."

—Borghild Lundberg Lee[15]

I. *Alien*

ALIEN

This reach of sagebrush with its windy hill
Framed by my doorway is a troubled place
I may have dreamed, or may be dreaming still—
A shifting world to flicker out in space.
And presently to cool azalea scents
And moonlight water I may wake once more—
To drifting swans with carven lineaments
That curve a silver arc along the shore.
And faintly now, I almost thought I heard—
As one would hear across the verge of sleep—
Out of the grey wind's sudden lull, in bars
Of gold the slender rapture of a bird—
A rift of joy that no wild throat could keep
Taking its flight among the listening stars.[16]

DESERT BORN

The forest straggles slowly to its death
Upon the desert's edge— and it was there
You flung your lusty joy to the first breath
Of sagebrush floating on the clear dry air.
Among the trees that crowded close as wheat,
The green gloom cast upon your heart a blight,
And made you restless for the vacant heat,
Eager to breast the shimmering flood of light.
For you were made for journeys in the sun,
And with the wind, the empty solitudes,
The world's bright borders only you are one;
This is your desert, with its strange vast moods,
You love it as wild things the secret glade—
You who are never lonely nor afraid.

THE DESERT

I

It will be spring upon the bare grey hills:
Across the sunny slopes will soon be seen,
Close in the wake of winter's lingering chills,
A trailing mist of thin ephemeral green.
Through this transparency the hills will be
Unmoved and grim, in scorn of compromise
With spring's brief carnival, inscrutably
Disdaining all her garments of disguise.
In frosty dawns the desert larks will pour
Their reckless flood of song upon this wide
Indifference; while under skies too clear
Old junipers, more weathered than before,
Grow wistful as they stand unglorified,
That May is but a shadow passing here.[17]

II

If there should come a wet wind from the sea
To freshen at the heart these hills that parch
Beneath the sun, or if more tenderly
The light should fall from the relenting arch
Above, if shadow cooled by rain should fold
Their broken rims in silver mist, subdue
And comfort them, their naked breasts might hold
The peace of forests, dim and veiled and blue.
The desert has its sorrows: dust for dreams
Of mist and trees to soften each contour
Too sharply drawn— of showers and of streams
Implacably withheld by some old foe;
And somewhere in these hills must still endure
A hunger such as only deserts know.

III

Autumn comes only to the desert skies
With flaming sunsets that too briefly burn
Above the sullen hills, a few faint cries
Of wild geese when the threatening dusks return.
Elsewhere October loiters with her dreams,
While wet boughs lift their crimson to the sun;
Elsewhere she scatters leaves on quiet streams
When all the golden ripening is done.
The naked grey expanses merely grow
More vast and chill. Like one who broods because
Of some old bitterness, some futile quest,
Some frustrate joy—forever doomed to show
A feigned impassiveness—the desert draws
The silence closer to its sterile breast.

IV

Compassionate through the lonely desert dark
A dream has come with chaste and gracious tread,
And junipers with branches warped and stark
Are lifting boughs of loveliness instead.
About the hollows and the nearest hill,
No longer tortured, with their bare scars gone—
Now that the solitary wind is still—
A white and healing silence has been drawn.
A dream has come to bring an interlude
Of beauty to the gloomy hills, to give
The trees their stainless grace against the sky;
Forgotten now, in this profound white mood,
How briefly an immaculate tree shall live,
How soon a sculptured marble hill must die.

Postponement

A mural, it might be, upon a wall—
A frescoed hill is not more fixed, unreal—
Its features bare, and yet inscrutable
With shadowy meanings it could well reveal.
Since a far, flaming birth gave this hill form,
With every desert rapture it is one,
Is ravaged by the mad wind and the storm
And by the passion of the desert sun.
From its dramatic stillness, I surmise,
That it has lived with self and sky and space—
That it has grown inured and grave and wise,
From porphyry sorrow chiselled on its face.
Yet with a fairer hill shall I delay,
Awaiting utterance . . . something it shall say?

II. *Wasteland*

Desert Hill

It does not change with any changing light—
The sunset flame, the tender tints of dawn—
Austere no less when they have touched its height,
Dispassionate alike when they are gone.
This hill has neither tree nor blade of grass
To sway and cool the winds as they go by,
To change or burn or fade as seasons pass—
It rises barren to the barren sky.
An ancient anguish that was fierce and tense
Might give this silence to its naked crest,
Its naked slopes this noble reticence,
Might give this granite quiet to its breast;
For wounds to which all healing is denied
There is indifference and lonely pride.

Late October

Autumn after autumn it shall know—
This passive mood that is so grey and still—
A thousand autumn days may come and go,
But never one shall gladden any hill.
No blue of river mist shall dim the gold
Of dreaming slopes when summer's song is done,
No maple's flaming rapture shall unfold
Above mown fields at peace beneath the sun.
Against the sky the patient junipers,
Across the lonely ridges dusty sage,
And in the hollows windy grass that stirs
And sighs,—this is the desert heritage.
But slumbering in this breast forever dumb,
May be an autumn that will never come.

DESERT FRUIT

Darkly above the rimrock's silhouette
In earth too sterile for a spruce or fir,
Obeying life's mysterious urge and fret,
It breasts the wind—this lonely juniper.
The meagre rains have slanted through its boughs
To pass like dreams of April—nothing more,
But never were there any birds to house,
And acrid berries all the fruit it bore;
A futile harvest which at length matured
Through two stern cycles of the desert year,
Two glassy seas of summer heat endured,
Two autumns with no soft enchantment here . . .
But from a desert ledge, what twisted root
Can bring its tree a golden-nectared fruit?

MIRAGE

Forgetful of the wide relentless heat
That wavers over flats of alkali,
Unmindful of betrayal and defeat,
The desert yields its vision to the sky.
Enchanted waters of a breathless blue
Whose dream waves lap upon a still dream shore,
And bending trees to their reflections true
Emerge from nothingness that went before.
Beauty is dreamed from pain in every land,
Is captured by the hand's most feeble might;
The burning desert only may command
Out of its doom, the miracle of light—
Only the bleaching desert, by its grace,
May dream its dream grown visible in space.

After Snow

As light as petals
From a shaken bough
The flakes were sifted
From the twilight sky;
The hill is hushed
With dawn upon its brow,
The hollows in
A white composure lie.

Unlike the drifted silence
Of a street,
That only for a season
Can withhold
The muffled traffic
That will come and go,
It lies unfurrowed here

By any feet,
Save of wild things
Made desolate by cold
That etch their furtive trails
Across the snow.

DESERT ROAD

The winding channel of the desert road
Between the sage, windswept and desolate,
Has made its course as water might have flowed
But turning never to a door nor gate.

Sands are forgetful, and a trail must bind
Some distant havens still, or disappear;
Nomadic wheels have kept this lane defined—
Men travel it but do not tarry here.

And sometimes in the sunset mystery
Of luminous dust along the golden span,
With phantom canvas gleaming, you may see
In cloudy shapes a moving caravan.[18]

THE LARK

The desert lark from the silver sage
Is singing in the sun!

The thirsty earth and air
Are drenched
In this bright rhapsody—
A sudden shower of notes that fall
Like raindrops shaken
From an April tree.

The dusty silence
Of the desert's heart
In reckless melody is drowned;
Upon the pallid quiet of its dreams
Is poured
A shining recompense of sound.

This waste whose sterile soil
Has never darkened
To a furrowing plough,
Is reaping rapture sweeter
Than the fruits of any bough.

SKETCH

Tilled land is a housewife
Gossiping across a wall;
The desert a slim gypsy
With a dagger in her shawl.

WILD STALLION

Gallop, gallop down the plain,
Nostrils wide and tossing mane!
Through the juniper, through the sage—
Fleet and proud your lineage.
Sweep and plunge— around— around—
Swifter, swifter drum the ground!
Let your black sides reach for breath,
Panting heart, you race with Death.

You are lithe and you are strong—
Rope is subtle, tight the thong.
Never halt to gaze or wonder,
Let your mad hoofs thunder, thunder!
Slacken not your frenzied pace,
For this, I fear, is your last race.

Proud horse, you are wind and flame,
From the trackless wild you came;
Deserts half a world apart
Mingle in your haughty heart.
Shall this blood then, cold and mute,
Lie about a rose's root?
A petal vein in deeper hue
Its velvet with the verve of you?
Shall this spirit live again
A rose scent in an English lane?

Wild heart, you are wind and sun!
Swifter, swifter—run—run!

III. *Sagebrush Village*

First April

His dog's sharp sudden bark upon the stillness
Will send me to the door with flying feet,
In that unguarded moment quite forgetting—
So wonted was this habit, and so sweet—
The empty vista through the swaying lilacs,
And out beyond the quiet village street.

Returning slowly to some threadbare duty,
Grown duller since the need for it has fled,
I ask how many journeys will betray me
Before I shall have learned to pause instead,
And make my foolish, dreaming heart remember
That he is dead— that he is dead![19]

Bequest

This was your dream, to give the desert song:
A lilac tree for April when it came;
A snowy clematis to glimmer long
Through summer dusks; for autumn days, the flame
Of maple leaves flung to the wind to mark
A gay surrender; and a poplar lane
To fortify your heart against the stark
And lonely reaches of the sky and plain.
The arid earth that lay inert and dumb
Awakened to your wistful touch and will,
To lift its fragile phrases guarded from
The noonday sun and wind, the evening chill . . .
And now spring tarries longer year by year
Because an exile with a dream was here.

Neighbor

She of the wild blood and the truant feet
That spurned dull paths, is now a prisoner
Within her four low walls. Her will was sweet
But homely needs have made a slave of her.
The brilliant golden plumage has been shed,
The restless hands that scorned a pan or seam
Are stained from serving him she chose, instead
Of many passing through her shoddy dream.
What man of them would think that love could tame
A wanton thus; that from the garish lights
Should bloom one shaded lamp; or that the blaze
Of dying fires should kindle this hearth's flame;
That from the feverish chaos of old nights
Should blossom forth these white and ordered days?

Spring Lamb

From cool and lofty pastures they have come,
A plaint of protest in each timid bleat,
But in the stifling air they have grown dumb,
Only their hoofs throb down the village street.

Above their heads a luminous cloud of dust
Refracts the desert sunlight and conceals
The harried band that sweeps on as it must,
A menace nipping ever at its heels.

And by some iron purpose driven on,
They have forsaken green and peaceful swales
For loading pens and the relentless dawn
That finds them launched upon the shining rails.

They go to a bleak fold. For I have heard
That from small huddled hoofs Death may descend—
Or if that woolly doom should be deferred,
He whets a welcome at the journey's end.

IV. *Silent Juniper*

WILD GEESE

In dark flight beating south they made
An etching thin and high—
I watched them in the early dusk
Go down the desert sky.

They left an arc of loneliness
To widen east and west,
An edge more piercing to the wind,
And winter in my breast.

One Autumn Night

With curtains drawn upon the desert night,
And one dim lamp a long-stemmed, yellow bloom
Against the dusk, the hearth-flame's echoed light
Shone faintly from the shadows of the room.
The quiet had its gracious way with me
Until, like sandaled feet upon a stair,
To thrill the silence with expectancy,
You came and stood a moment by my chair.
Into the dark an unrelenting door
Stood wide at last, and could not now deter
Your step. You came, responsive to a call
Grown old, but ineffectual no more;
You came, lured from beyond what barrier,
You who in life would never come at all!

Release

By dreams deserted,
My heart is old—
A winter forest
Still and cold.

Even sorrow
That I keep,
Is a frozen river
In lonely sleep.[20]

Finale [Desert]

And now that I have come to days
Whose quiet is unstirred
And strangely new,
Too quiet and too strange
Is this chill peace
That holds no swift
Bewilderment of you.

Remembering so
The wild wind sweeping by,
A lonely old tree grieves
Through long December silences
For the lost rapture
Of its shaken leaves.[21]

Silent Juniper

Yes, I am lonely . . . but I know a tree
That stands alone upon a grey hill's crest,
The reach about it empty as the sea,
The waste winds bitter from the east and west.
To this dark tree the seasons come and go
But bring no white bloom nor a burning leaf—
By its grim foliage you would never know
That sometimes, passionate and mute and brief,
The spring is at its heart. And once betrayed
By wings too eager or a flight too long,
A bright bird came to rest within its shade,
And turned the morning golden with his song . . .
Songs live in fairer trees from sun to sun—
The silent juniper remembers one.[22]

V. *Desert Songs*

DESERT SONGS

I

There may be hills beyond these ridges
Whose breasts have only scars to show;
There may be hills by mist enchanted—
I do not know.

There may be sound beyond this silence—
A wind through leaves to sing and dream,
And birdnotes that are glints of sunlight
Upon the surface of the stream.

There may be peace of quiet water
To echo clouds that drift through space;
There may be paths through alder thickets,
And shadows that would cool my face.

There may be hills as blue as evening,
And slowly ripening fields below,
Somewhere beyond these futile reaches—
I do not know.

II

A path would call me if it could
Across a field and through the wood—
A path of shadow to beguile
My footsteps down its dusky aisle.

And gladly, gladly I should go
By the willows bending low,
With their silver boughs at rest
On the water's limpid breast.

A quiet wind would cool my face
In that leafy, sheltered place,
Where the yielding earth lay deep
In a peace that I should keep . . .

But I shall follow in my dream
The willow path beside the stream,
While still this blinding desert heat
Upon my head will beat, will beat!

III

Cool dreams come from the silences
Like wind over the sea
And like the wind are gone;
Cool dreams over the barren hills,
Over the fragrant sage,
Blow fresh from every dawn.

IV

They do not change, these high horizons,
These wastes more lonely than the sea,
Unbrightened by the glint of water,
By snowy bough or crimson tree.

Beneath the chastening winds the desert
Lifts to the sun its sterile breast,
An unspent heart that dreams of gardens,
And fields by warm green rains caressed.

Sunset will come, a stately prelude,
The dark will cover cruel scars;
After the wind the velvet quiet,
The cool compassion of the stars.

V

If I should fall beside the sea,
At last with its blue rapture spent,
Dreaming of white gulls I shall lie
Utterly content.

Or if the forest has its way,
Its hushed green cadences will sweep
To deeper quiet my stilled heart—
And I shall sleep . . .

But if I sink to silences
More bitter for the waste wind's stir,
I shall creep back to life again
A wistful juniper.

VI. *The Desert Wife*

The Desert Wife

I

They crossed the final mountain in their path,
A lofty rampart with a weathered peak,
Like a forbidding god enthroned, whose wrath
Would halt the timid and deter the weak.
The two had come by perilous strands of road
Festooned like cobwebs up the mountain side—
He drove his own team in the country's mode,
And she beside him but three days a bride.
Hills beyond hills she saw, tier after tier,
With desolate rounded crests as bare as stone,
And lost in this wild chaos, far or near,
Were the few acres they would call their own.
With heart dismayed her lips pressed back a cry—
His face was forward and his chin was high.

There was no water, but the soil was good,
With sagebrush higher than a tall man's shoulder;
Such land would make a farm if any would,
And that, he said, before they were much older.
She helped him build the shack beneath the hill—
In her own way— for every flimsy rafter
Went up, the doors were fitted, every sill
Was nailed to snatches of her song and laughter.
He carted water, till the well was dug,
From the warm spring three miles or more away,
And her slim hands with drapery or rug
Were busy, but her recreant thoughts would stray;
For fields and orchards she could not forget,
Often in secret her blue eyes were wet.

III

They had their dreams of green alfalfa fields
With thriving growths to cut— and lusty clover,
Of yellow acres and their yellow yields
To fill their granaries and brim them over.
Seasons would follow— summer follow spring
As orderly as in a gentler place;
By sowing and by reaping they might bring
Time to a desert that had known but space.
They would diminish with their poplar trees
Horizons that were too remote and vast,
Surround the house and garden, and from these
Bar out primeval loneliness at last . . .
She must have trees against the hill, she said,
That frowned unbearably upon her head.

Meanwhile he fenced, prepared the soil for seed—
He had that passion for the earth that spares
No pains—he laughed at toil—such was his breed—
In three years more the homestead would be theirs.
Urged by her love of home, with him to please,
She worked as early at her tasks, and late;
She helped him carry water for the trees,
And made a garden that the gophers ate;
And sometimes in the need of change from labor,
Snake-stick in hand, she vanished down the trail
To get a start of yeast, or ask her neighbor
The proper way to cook a cotton-tail.
For something warm and intimate on the mat,
He brought a white dog and a yellow cat.

V

She learned the seasons not from shaping leaf,
Not from a sombre, unshed foliage,
But from the creatures of the wild in brief
Excursion down her vast and windy stage.
Of hurrying birds, not many paused to sing,
Save one bright tenant, the elusive lark—
In his exultant note she heard the spring,
Heard autumn call with wild geese in the dark.
She shared the secrets of her solitude,
Was stricken at the downfall of a swan,
Found with delight a sage hen's cheeping brood,
Grew rapt to glimpse an antelope and fawn . . .
Time came when any wild thing with its young
Would set her musing with a silent tongue.

VI

A desert's subtlety was known that year
In gossamer rains of silver tissue spun,
That scarcely touched the earth to disappear
As vapour curling upward in the sun;
Marked in the cool mirage with lakes of blue,
A taunting dream that perished on the air,
And in the snow's brief beauty that withdrew
To leave the hills again to grey despair.
One snow was deep, and rabbits reaching higher,
More starved than usual, the natives said,
Girdled the bark above the bands of wire,
And in the spring they found their trees were dead.
The wind blew dust to make her cleaning vain,
But never any downpour for the grain.

VII

How quaint the fashions were, the gowns so slim!
How would they look, she wondered to the dog,
And could she wear a hat so close and trim?—
Turning the pages of a catalogue.
Her heart went yearning to another scene,
Down lighted thoroughfares of her desire,
But sighing for the lava-miles between,
She muted her dreams to tend the sagebrush fire.
The crops had failed again—if they could go . . .
He shook his head and said he meant to stay,
Might build a dam to catch the melting snow,
Expected yet to raise a stand of hay.
And to his will hers must be reconciled—
It would be better when she had the child.

VIII

Strange that a hill that was so stark and bare
Could harbor mystery at its cinder core—
Curious she should sense it ever there
Baffling and sinister beyond her door.
And terrible to her an ultimate power
As still as this, and ages gathering,
That seemed to wait for some unguarded hour
Crouched like a tawny beast about to spring;
A menace that was more impending still,
And laid upon her heart a deeper fear,
When from the ghostly moon mist the stark hill
Took voice in protest to their presence here—
Cried through the weird coyote's midnight bark
And sent her to his pillow in the dark.

Nature had curved her warm lips into smiles,
The brightness of the sun was in her hair—
A stout heart often for a space beguiles
A breast too delicate to nourish care.
Her hands had widened and her slender feet
Had slowed their lilting tempo to a plod;
If flesh complained she had but to repeat
That her mother's mother's first house was of sod.
The child was ailing, toil had quenched her song,
She suddenly perceived that she was old—
That life was but two seasons, brief or long,
Summer and winter only, heat or cold;
Two seasons marched across the desert page—
Summer and winter, girlhood and old age.

X

If roads were passable they drove to town,
Her high adventure once or twice a year;
(To climb the rocky summit and then down
Made miles too many when his time was dear).
A store, a church, a barn with empty stalls,
A dozen houses in this oasis,
With families sheltered by their drunken walls,
Made it for her a fair metropolis.
But more than talk of women she had craved,
Than piles of bright prints on the shelves—far more—
She loved a battered lilac that had braved
The desert drought and grew beside a door—
The dusty scent hat quickened in her breast
Something she thought had perished with the rest.

It had no need of them, this silent land,
From its ungracious mood no word to say,
Asked nothing of the lonely alien hand,
With nothing it could add or take away.
What to each separate eternity
The daily growth of an ambiguous vine?
What to a desert was a blossoming tree
When it was finished to each classic line?
And what of these long years of fruitless toil
To be unsanctioned at the end, unblest?
Not like the friendly watered land, this soil
Would never take tired children to its breast;
To their irrelevant, half-wistful trust
Had made its answer in a swirl of dust.

They grew more passive with the meagre years,
Upon their lips and hearts the desert lay
The silence that had throbbed upon their ears—
And after all there was not much to say.
Disheartened neighbors vanished one by one,
A hill grave claimed the last child of the four,
She watched the sagebrush billow in the sun,
A lonelier exile on a lonelier shore.
Then life so long a tread of weariness
Waned suddenly, perhaps to her surprise,
And one blue-aproned, faded woman less
Stared from a door with hunger in her eyes . . .
And he surrendered what faith he had kept
To an empty kitchen and a hearth unswept.

XIII

Only a wall is left . . . the fallen frame
Lies like a bleached and scattered skeleton,
And they who thought to build and to reclaim
Are gone, as wilder tribes have come and gone.
With sun and wind across the burning sand,
The desert ruthlessly has taken all
That marked their brief intrusion save a strand
Of sagging fence, a reach of silvered wall.
Indifferent and timeless as the stars,
Few are the records it will not erase—
The futile footprints and the surface scars
Of men too puny for its light and space.
From age to age the waste shall brood and dream,
Mysterious and silent and supreme.

POEMS
1933–1955

Summer's End

These leaves of gold that lie about my feet
With dawns and sunsets gone no more contend—
Lost loveliness, a span at last complete,
A rapture finished to the flaming end.
From April bud this beauty strewn has made
A season's growth, unlike the leaves that cling
In blackened tatters to a tree betrayed,
And left frost-stricken in the midst of spring.
Love, too, has both its green and barren bough—
And when these leaves are blown across the hill
And scattered by the winds that stir them now,
In greater girth, more deeply rooted still,
This tree will lift its naked branches high—
So, stripped of love, I face the winter sky.

Sunday Oregonian, November 12, 1933

Mission Garden

The patio is stilled beneath the sun,
A place long since enchanted it might be;
A haze of color from the summers gone.
It mellows in its own tranquility.
The ruined campanario whose chimes
Are hushed, the shadows that are never blurred
Nor lengthened on the flags, the ancient limes,
The magic fountain, and the fabled bird
Long since were charmed, and left to sun and dreams
These hundred years between the crumbling walls;
Yet less a place perceived, this garden seems,
Than something that a groping mind recalls—
The ending of an unacknowledged quest,
A memory that lingers in my breast.[23]

North Carolina Poetry Review, April 1934

AFTERNOON

(San Juan Capistrano)

But to this garden will my heart return—
Its autumns grieve for this eternal spring,
To this sweet sunshine will its darkness yearn,
Its silences will hear a linnet sing;
Not for the beauty of the ruined wall,
The crumbling cloisters where the ivy creeps,
The sun-scented stocks—beyond them all
Is something more than beauty that it keeps.

A century of afternoons like these—
Of bells to peal and pepper boughs to sway,
Of swallows soaring high above the trees,
And patient feet to groove the tiles of clay—
Their golden essence yielded one by one,
A hundred years are dreaming in the sun.

Sunday Oregonian, April 1, 1934

LOVE

My stately new candle
In white splendor stands;
Its flame shall be sheltered
In my curved hands.

No wind must discover
This warm hidden light,
Or I shall be groping
Again through the night.

Pictorial Review, April 1935

AFTERNOON

(Spanish Southwest)

The patio is stilled beneath the sun,
A place long since enchanted, it might be;
A haze of colors from the summers gone,
It mellows in its own tranquility.
The ruined campanario whose chimes
Are hushed, the prints of leaves that lie unstirred
For ages on the flags, the ancient limes
The magic fountain and the fabled bird
Long since were charmed and left to sun and dreams
These hundred years between the crumbling walls;
Yet less a place perceived, this garden seems,
Than something that a groping mind recalls—
The ending of an unacknowledged quest,
A memory that lingers in my breast.

Sunday Oregonian, October 6, 1935
Oregonian, January 3, 1940

They Do Not Know

They say that you will leave,
As lovers do,
A row of blighted days
Once white with you.

They do not know that now
I shall not care
How swift the wind—the wind that sweeps
My garden bare.

This season, too, can swing
Through a brief arc.
If I may take its sun
Into the dark.

If I may take its song—
Shaped softly then—
Under my quiet hands
To earth again.

Sunday Oregonian, October 29, 1933

EBB-TIDE

And now I yield
And let the sea
Draw its grey peace
Over me.

The pulse of time
At last is still;
My world a beach
below a hill.

Inert upon
The clean cool sand
I do not move
A foot or hand.

And I have neither
Grief nor pride—
The thongs of life
Have come untied.

Concerned alone
With wind and spray—
Of flesh and mind
No longer prey. . .

Save by the sea,
Where can I lie,
As deep and empty
As the sky? [24]

Henry Harrison, *Oregon Poets*, 1935

NOCTURNE

Midnight . . . and wind that is southwardly shifting
To lure from the orchard the fragrance it brings;
Midnight . . . with draperies over you drifting,
Light as the stir of invisible wings;
Midnight . . . and out of the hush your soft breathing
Rises and falls in a rhythmic beat,
While the faint smile that your warm lips are wreathing
Tells of a dream that is sweet.

Sleep . . . while the moonbeams are silently stealing
On cool silver feet through the dusk of the room;
Sleep . . . while they linger beside you revealing
A night-folded flower, your face in the gloom;
Sleep . . . while I watch here, nor know in your dreaming
How I am held by the shadow of dread—
Dread of some midnight with clear moonlight streaming
Down the empty white aisle of your bed.[25]

Henry Harrison, *Oregon Poets,* 1935

Spring Night

Twilight has faded, but whitely the iris,
Whitely the hawthorn blossoms glow;
Mystical, stately, the swans are drifting
White as our dreams on the lake below.

Leaves in the starlight, leaves on the water,
Aprils have patterned them, autumns shall reap;
Beauty of earth remembered, forgotten,
This is the hour my heart shall keep.[26]

Good Housekeeping, April 1936

THEN APRIL

I saw the silent golden leaves
Fall from the autumn pear,
With sorrow for a summer's end,
A bough of love left bare.

And through the gray of winter days,
Unwinding like a thread,
My heart knew peace as it is known
Among the dreamless dead.

But these things brought life throbbing back
With a swift stab of pain—
Wet fragrance from a lilac tree,
A bird-song through the rain.[27]

Good Housekeeping, April 1937

FINALE

(Old Front Street)

No sounds disturb, no traffic tides confuse
These precincts of the past that lie apart;
Forsaken streets, forgotten avenues,
A city slumbering in a city's heart.
Six decades linger in the silent square,
The fountain's silver falls on sculptured stone;
Victorian charm, an uninvaded air—
For their surrender nothing shall atone.

They who would keep old beauty and its spell,
And stay the restless hand that spares it not,
Find change a sorrow that they bear not well
But Athens crumbles, dust is Camelot;
The Bridge of London falls in time's morass,
For all is mutable, and all must pass.

Spectator, June 1941

To the *Oregon*

She lies forgotten on a coral strand,
A bleaching wreck beneath a tropic sun,
A proud ship humbled, under no command,
Shorn of her might, doomed to oblivion.
She lies rejected on an island shore,
Unworthy now to conquer or defend,
To sail the glorious voyages that bore
The valiant ship to this inglorious end.

Lonely the harbor is for the great ship,
Lonely the sky for her familiar spars;
No more at sunset will her colors dip,
Her noble hull loom dark against the stars.
Farewell, old ship, a very long farewell!
Our venerations failed, love could not save;
We keep the memory, though we hear the knell,
Brave ships die not, nor sink beneath the wave.

Immortal ship, join that immortal fleet
That Time has launched upon the fateful tides!
Sail seas beyond destruction and defeat,
While past your berth the silent river glides![28]

Sunday Oregonian, September 30, 1945

Sleep Song

Of greening bough, of the misty hill,
Of the dogwood tree, and the grassy sweep,
Of the sudden wind on the daffodil,
Dream not. Dream not of April. Sleep!

On pools of jade let the lilies float,
And the willow over the pale stream weep,
The fountain's murmuring grow remote,
Of morning sun no memory keep;
To petal drift and the robin's note,
Awaken not. In silence, sleep.

The song is lost with the vanished wing,
Bare is the bough, and the sorrow deep,
The music dies with the broken string,
The requiem wind is singing . . . Sleep.

Sunday Oregonian, May 2, 1948

Indian Summer

Blue valley haze and amber sunlight reign,
Unburdened orchard trees no longer bend,
Gone from the fields the swaying yellow grain,
The seed to earth and growth is at an end.
The energy that brought the russet fruit
To hang in ripe perfection from the tree,
The life resurgent upward from the root
Recedes, an ebbing tide to the dark sea.
Forgotten in this golden mood is spring,
The ruthless storms of blossoms long since lost.
The coming of grey dusks, the migrant wing,
The imminence of brittle flowers of frost—
This mellow mood that holds no fear or fret,
Dread of December, for April no regret.

Oregonian, October 12, 1953

Holiday

Do you remember lilies drifting on the pool,
Sampans, you called them, on a summer sea;
Imaged in water made twice beautiful,
Imagined in water the enchanted tree?
The ancient turtle that beguiled the hours,
The black swans black reflections as in glass,
Do you remember sudden petal showers,
The shadows lengthening slowly on the grass? . . .
The golden afternoon that reached an end
On wings that cast no faint, penumbrous dread,
The moment marked for parting friend from friend,
The moment when our gay goodbyes were said—
Waving farewell to meet on some tomorrow,
Waving a hand to Death, a hand to Sorrow?

Sunday Oregonian (Northwest ROTO Magazine),
August 22, 1954

INVASION

Who shall deliver the desert,
This waste of sand and sage
From the demon that rides the wind
In an armor of dust?
Who shall deliver the gray and seasonless land,
Captive to its own desolation?
Who shall prevail against the evil
That guards the barren scarp and cliff,
The remoteness, the silence, from day to day,
The loneliness, the death? . . .
None shall prevail against the spirit
That dwells in these sterile expanses,
Ever watchful, ever suspicious, ever unfriendly.
Only the silver ripple of water
Moving through narrow channels carries defeat,
The demon of the waste is a gray shadow
That flees to the hills
Before the sweet laughter of water.

Sunday Oregonian, October 24, 1954

ANOTHER HARVEST

The harvest's ended, garnered are the sheaves,
And now the field is lonely for the grain,
Shorn to the aching stubble, it still grieves
Beneath the sun, beneath the autumn rain.
The sickle passed too quickly, taking all,
Too swiftly summer fell before the blade;
And never can the power of earth recall
The rippling gold, now severed and betrayed.
Dark in the stubble lies the empty field,
The winds of autumn sweep it without sound;
It waits, until the snows of winter yield
To meadowlarks above the harrowed ground,
To spears of spring, again the crested gold—
Another harvest from the silent mold.

Sunday Oregonian, (Northwest ROTO Magazine),
November 14, 1954

Desert Mountain

To barren heights, they rise, these slopes of gray,
Wind-scarred through every season of the year;
Unchanged by any growths or trees of May,
The solitary slopes of bleak Bendire.
Not from this ashen soil are meadows born
To flourish greenly through the early spring,
Not for this summit that the winds have worn
Is any swaying branch or folded wing.
Evening may bring vast color from the west,
When light descending sweeps the Olympian brow,
And hues of heaven touch the granite breast,
When purple shadows deepen to allow
A moment's beauty from gray centuries won.[29]

Sunday Oregonian, March 13, 1955

Afterword

Of all the early Oregon poets I discovered during my two years of research for the Oregon poetry anthology *From Here We Speak* (Oregon State University Press, 1994), none touched me more deeply, or surprised me more happily, than Ada Hastings Hedges and her brilliant work.

Here was a poet whose technical skills were equal to and beyond those of most of her peers, of whatever gender, and her fierceness of spirit, lack of sentimentality, and complex vision placed her, in my estimation, among the best poets writing anywhere in the United States in the first part of the twentieth century—as demonstrated by the many prestigious journals that published her individual poems.

And yet in her lifetime, she saw just a single full-length collection of her work—the result, perhaps, of lack of time and good connections, but also (I strongly suspect) because most poetry book publishers were still located east of the Mississippi, where prejudice against writers from "the West," and especially against women writers, was the norm.

So, when I first learned of this book, still in the making, and of the dedication to Hedges's work and the tremendous, years-long efforts that Alan Contreras and Ulrich Hardt had invested in collecting these poems, I was, as the current saying goes, "beyond thrilled" and oh, so grateful. To these coeditors I send my everlasting thanks and most heartfelt applause.

Thanks and applause, also, to OSU Press! Due to the good taste and discernment of Tom Booth, director, and the publication team—acquisitions editor Kim Hogeland; editorial, design, and production manager Micki Reaman; and marketing manager Marty Brown, you—lucky reader—hold in your hands not only a visually stunning book, but one whose relevance and power will endure. It will touch your hearts.

"All poetry is regional, somewhere," William Stafford once wrote—and the "regional" poems of Ada Hastings Hedges, which encompass both the eastern and the western parts of our state, making her a perfect fit for OSU Press, also have the philosophical breadth and complexity of perspective that will stand the test of time and will have a universal appeal.

Their value is also historical: publication of this book will fill some notable gaps on library shelves, both in Oregon and beyond, of 1) poetry that draws specifically on the Oregon landscape, especially that east of the Cascades; 2) outstanding poetry from the first half of the twentieth century; 3) poetry that teachers will love teaching and students will not only tolerate but enjoy, filled as it is with paradox and utterly fresh, extended metaphor; 4) poetry in which readers can find themselves and their own, complex lives and emotions; and 5) poetry by formidable women poets active, in the United States, during the first half of the twentieth century.

To readers wary of meter and rhyme (having, like me, endured lots of sing-song stuff), I say give these poems a chance. They're different. Seldom, if ever, are Hedges's rhymes predictable. Yes, they rhyme, but they are also poems of rebellion, of breaking with traditional expectations. The rhymes work together with the words to rub up against, while working within, the limitations of both poetic form and social convention, and that gives the poems a delightful and powerful "edge." That "edge" drives them forward. And the music within individual lines gives them the quality of "the memorable" that will stay with us, much as we remember certain lines of our own favorite poets, including Shakespeare.

But what I most admire and love in the work of Ada Hastings Hedges—apart from fresh employment of conventional forms—is the poet's brave, unsentimental, and uncompromising recognition of "the wide indifference" of the natural world to human concerns, accompanied by her dogged determination to keep "dreaming beauty from every land."

In times like our own, where the fragility of our planet is being tested and compromised every day, with always a new extinction on its way, along with the next raging fire or hurricane—I need poems that honor and remind me of the small things that still survive and can bring small moments of joy and wonder to our everyday lives, moments that keep us going and renew our souls.

When Hedges writes of "the slender rapture of a bird," I think of the rapture we can hear in her own finely crafted lines, each one, to my ears, a "rift of joy that no wild throat could keep / Taking its flight among the listening stars."

These poems are meant to be read aloud. Read them to an empty room, read them to friends. Their echoes will stay with you, reader, long after your book is closed.

Ingrid Wendt
Eugene, Oregon
October 2019

Notes

ACKNOWLEDGMENTS

1   See Ingrid Wendt and Primus St. John, eds. *From Here We Speak: An Anthology of Oregon Poetry* (Corvallis: Oregon State University Press, 1993).

INTRODUCTION

1   Includes material adapted and expanded from Hardt's *Oregon Encyclopedia* entry on Hedges.

2   *Oregon Journal*, February 25, 1925, 5.

3   *Sunday Oregonian*, July 14, 1935, 6.

4   *Sunday Oregon Journal*, November 20, 1938, 9.

5   "Wings of the Morning," *Albany Democrat*, January 11, 1925, 5.

6   Alfred Powers, *History of Oregon Literature* (Portland, OR: Metropolitan Press, 1935), 651–652.

7   Ethel Romig Fuller, "Who and How Good Are Oregon Poets?" *Sunday Oregonian*, November 19, 1933, 6. The lines of poetry are from "The Desert II."

8   *Sunday Oregon Journal*, November 1, 1925, 6.

9   *Sunday Oregon Journal*, November 1, 1925, 6. "The Desert III" is a later version of the poem "Autumn in the Desert," first published in *Contemporary Verse*, as quoted by Corning in this article.

10 Howard McKinley Corning, "Portraiture of Life Seen as Vindication of Poetry," *Sunday Oregonian*, December 6, 1925, 2.

11 Ethel Romig Fuller, "Preface," *Oregon Poets: An Anthology of 50 Contemporaries* (New York: Henry Harrison, 1935), n.p.

12 Rufus A. Coleman, ed. *Northwest Books* (Portland, OR: Binfords & Mort, 1942).

13 Frederick Woodward Skiff, *Landmarks and Literature: An American Travelogue* (Portland, OR: Metropolitan Press, Publishers, 1937).

14 Borghild Lundberg Lee, *Sunday Oregon Journal*, March 14, 1926, 6.

15 Borghild Lundberg Lee, *Spectator*, November 1933.

16 Howard McKinley Corning, "Charles Alexander: Youth of the Oregon Mood," *Oregon Historical Quarterly* 74, no. 1 (March 1973): 34–70. Quoted passage from p. 58.

17 Stewart H. Holbrook, *Promised Land: A Collection of Northwest Writing* (New York: McGraw-Hill, 1945), xiv–xv.

18 *Oregon Sunday Journal*, March 14, 1926, 6.

19 Robert C. Pooley, et al., *The United States in Literature* (Chicago: Scott, Foresman & Co., 2017).

Poems

1   "Sanctuary" is thought to be Hedges's first published poem. It is credited to Ada M. Hedges, but that appears to be simply a reference to her middle name, May, as the style is clearly hers, and she published several early poems as Ada M. Hedges.

2   In "If You Had Died," the word "flowingtide" is unbroken in the original printed version. This may be an error, and the editors have chosen to split the words here. The first two words are capitalized in the printed original, which may have been the publisher's choice. The second line indent is in the original. In the reprinted version, there is no capitalization or indentation, and "flowing tide" is two words.

3   Book editor Gwladys Bowen selected "Captivity" and the following two poems for the second week of her new column, "Poets' Corner," in the *Sunday Oregon Journal*, an indication of the prominent place Hedges occupied among contemporary poets. The newspaper published the poet's residential address with the poem, a practice dropped the following month.

4   The subtitle was added to "Farewell" for purposes of this volume. Although our only source for this poem is Viola Price Franklin's *A Tribute to Hazel Hall*, published by Caxton Printers (Caldwell, Idaho) in 1939, the context of the poem is clearly the period after poet Hazel Hall's death (May 11, 1924), so we have placed it here in sequence.

5   A quite different five-stanza version of "Sleep, Stay Your Feet" appeared in the *New York Times* on July 21, 1927. See page 34. Line 14, "Let others stray," was not indented in the original publication of the poem.

6   "Resurgence" was reprinted in *Defiance Crescent-News*, Defiance, Ohio, May 25, 1925. The poem won "best sonnet of the year" award from *Muse & Mirror* in 1924.

7   A very different three-stanza poem, also entitled "Then April," appeared in *Good Housekeeping* in April 1937. See page 124.

8   This first version of "Finale" has a different layout and wording from the "Finale" that appeared in *Desert Poems* in 1930. See p. 86.

9 The last line of "Alien (Whenever April walks)" was not indented in the original publication.

10 A quite different version of "Alien (The reach of sagebrush)" appeared as the opening poem in *Desert Poems* in 1930. See p. 55.

11 In the original published version of "Sleep, Stay Your Step," line 14, "Find grief laid bare," is not indented. This may be an error. The editors have chosen to indent it here. An earlier and quite different four-stanza version of this poem, entitled "Sleep, Stay Your Feet," appeared in the *Sunday Oregon Journal*, February 15, 1925. See p. 34.

12 The last line of "Bequest" is not indented in the original published version. An extensively reworked version under the same title appeared in *Desert Poems*. See page 78.

13 "Now" was originally published in *Poetry* 31, no. 2 (November 1927): 79. Reprinted under the title "This Hour" in Henry Harrison, *Oregon Poets* (1935):67 with the word "whose" dropped from the line "But for this flesh whose pulses beat." This appears to be an error, as the line does not scan properly in Harrison.

14 "Mist" was originally published in the *Commonweal*, October 1928. Reprinted in Henry Harrison, *Oregon Poets* (1935):67. Different words appear in that version, shown here in bold:

> . . .
>
> Like **gladness** time has reaped, the soft mist holds
>
> . . .
>
> **The mist that keeps the shaken soul secure**
> **From more of rapture than it could endure.**

15 The epigraph is from Borghild Lundberg Lee's review of *Desert Poems* in the *Spectator*, November 18, 1933. This comment refers to "The Desert Wife."

16 A quite different version of "Alien" appeared in the *Commonweal*, June 9, 1926. See p. 44.

17 "The Desert" was reprinted in *Northwest Literary Review* 1, no. 1 (May–June, 1935): 9. An earlier version appeared as "Desert Spring" in the *Nation*, April 17, 1929. Different wording in that version is shown in boldface below:

> **Remote** and grim, in scorn of compromise
>
> . . .
>
> In frosty dawns the **meadow** larks will pour
>
> . . .
>
> Indifference; while under [*the*] skies too clear

18 "Desert Road" was reprinted in *Northwest Literary Review* 1, no. 4 (November–December, 1935): 5.

19 "First April" originally appeared with the title "Solus" in *Lyric West*, December 1924. Reprinted in the *Sunday Albany Democrat*, January

18, 1925, and in *Anthology of Magazine Verse for 1925* and *Yearbook of American Poetry*, 1925.

20 "Release" was originally published in *Poetry* 31, no. 2 (November 1927): 79.

21 The word "Desert" has been added to the title of "Finale" by the editors, to distinguish this poem from an earlier version published in the *Sunday Oregon Journal* on November 1925. See p. 41. A quite different poem entitled "Finale (Old Front Street)" was published in the *Spectator* in 1941. See p. 125.

22 "Silent Juniper" was reprinted in Henry Harrison, *Oregon Poets* (1935): 68. See p. 87.

23 Originally published in *North Carolina Poetry Review* 1, no. 10 (April 1934): 77. A later version of "Mission Garden" was published under the title "Afternoon (Spanish Southwest)" in the *Oregonian*. See p. 119.

24 An earlier source for "Ebb-Tide" probably exists but was not located.

25 An earlier source for "Nocturne" probably exists but was not located.

26 In the original appearance of "Spring Night," the first word of each stanza is capitalized, which is more likely an artifact of the publisher's choice than of the poet's. This poem was set to music by Margaret Hyde Winters.

27 In the original appearance of "Then April," the first word of each stanza is capitalized, which is more likely an artifact of the publisher's choice than of the poet's. A very different version, "Then April!," was published in the *Sunday Oregon Journal*, April 4, 1925: 5. See page 36.

28 The battleship USS *Oregon* was an iconic vessel of the Spanish-American war, known for its dash around South America in 1898, just in time to play a decisive role in the battle of Santiago de Cuba. The scene depicted in "To the *Oregon*" and in the accompanying illustration appears to show the ship's hull being used as a dynamite barge in the closing months of WWII. Its mast is in the Tom McCall Waterfront Park in Portland. See Bert Webber, *Battleship Oregon* (1994) for a thorough, well-illustrated story of the ship. The last line is italic in the original.

29 In "Desert Mountain," the reference to "bleak Bendire"—rhymes with "year"—is undoubtedly to sage-covered Bendire Mountain, about twenty miles north of Juntura, Malheur County, Oregon, where Hedges lived for over a decade. The peak is named for Major Charles E. Bendire, a military doctor and early ornithologist in the region. This poem was published thirty-three years after Hedges left Juntura, when she was seventy-one. This is the last published poem that the editors could locate.

Bibliography

Allen, Eleanor. "Oregon Becomes Active Center for Writers." *Sunday Oregonian* (March 29, 1936): 58.

Coleman, Rufus Arthur. *Northwest Books, Report of the Inland Empire Council of Teachers of English*, 2nd ed. Portland, OR: Binfords & Mort, 1942.

Corning, Howard McKinley. "Charles Alexander: Youth of the Oregon Mood," *Oregon Historical Quarterly*, 74.1 (March 1973): 34-70.

Fuller, Ethel Romig. "Who and How Good Are Oregon Poets?" *Sunday Oregonian* (November 19, 1933): 6.

Hardt, Ulrich H. *The Oregon Encyclopedia of History and Culture*. Entry: Ada Hastings Hedges, 2018.

Harrison, Henry, ed. *Oregon Poets: An Anthology of 50 Contemporaries.* New York: Henry Harrison, 1935.

Hedges, Ada Hastings. *Desert Poems.* Portland, OR: Metropolitan Press, Publishers, 1930.

Holbrook, Stewart H., ed. *Promised Land: A Collection of Northwest Writing.* New York: McGraw-Hill Book Co., 1945.

Lee, Borghild Lundberg. "Mrs. Hedges Is Exquisite Artist in Her Poetry." *Oregon Journal* (March 14, 1926), sec. 4: 6.

Mansfield, Margery, ed. *American Women Poets 1937.* New York: Henry Harrison, 1937.

"New Books of Poetry" [review of *Desert Poems*]. *New York Times* (March 1, 1931): BR 10.

Pooley, Robert C., et al., eds. *The United States in Literature.* Chicago: Scott, Foresman & Co., 2017.

Powers, Alfred. *History of Oregon Literature.* Portland, OR: Metropolitan Press, Publishers, 1935.

Skiff, Frederick Woodward. *Landmarks and Literature: An American Travelogue.* Portland, OR: Metropolitan Press, Publishers, 1937.

Skinner, Jeremy. *The Binfords and Mort Publishing Company and the Development of Regional Literature in Oregon.* Portland State University, Dissertations and Theses, 2011.

Venn, George. "Where the Crooked River Rises: A High Desert Home" (book review), *Oregon Historical Quarterly,* 112.2 (Summer 2011): 268–269.

Webber, Bert. *Battleship Oregon: Bulldog of the Navy.* Medford, OR: Webb Research Group, 1994.

Wendt, Ingrid, and Primus St. John, eds. *From Here We Speak: An Anthology of Oregon Poetry.* Corvallis, OR: Oregon State University Press, 1993.

Index of Titles

Index of First Lines